THE CONCISE HA...
COUNTRY...
FLAGS, FACTS & STATS OF C...
202...

CONTENTS

FEATURES & NOTES

- **Tabbed alphabetical indexing** quickly search your desired country using the bled-to-edge alphabetical tabs showing the countries included in any double page spread.

- **Country location maps** search your desired country on the included world map using the numbered system. Each country is assigned a number which can be matched with a numbered label on the map in any double page spread.

- **Country stat rankings** see how your desired country ranks of all countries in the world for area, population, GDP and highest point with a ranking displayed after the country facts.

- **Extended country data** as well as the 7 country facts, the continent, country name by the country's language (e.g. Deutschland for Germany) and majority religious affiliation as efficiently displayed alongside the country name.

- **Data** was collected from online sources such as the IMF, Wikipedia and the CIA world factbook. Data for country stats exclude country dependencies and self-governing states, such as Greenland to Denmark. All data was correct at time of collection. **'Area'** is the total size of a country including territorial waters. **'GDP'** is the nominal gross domestic product of a country. **'Official Language'** is a special-status language of a country, often used by government, which may differ from a widely used language. Languages in () are national languages (widely used) where an official language is not defined. Majority **religious** affiliation is displayed using a symbol below. Countries with 2 majority religions (within 10%) have 2 symbols.

  Islam Christianity Judaism Buddhism Hinduism Atheism FOLK Folk Religion

- **Credits:** MapChart for world map graphics.

B.C. Lester Books
Geography publications for the people since 2019.

Visit us at www.bclesterbooks.com for more!

A QUICK MESSAGE FROM THE AUTHOR

THANKS FOR PURCHASING THIS BOOK...

...we really hope you enjoy it. If you have the chance, then all feedback on Amazon is greatly appreciated. We have put a lot of effort into making this book, so if you are not completely satisfied, please email us at ben@bclesterbooks.com and we will do our best to address any issues. If you have any suggestions, want to get in touch or send us a selfie with this book, then email at the same address - ben@bclesterbooks.com

Is this book misprinted? Printing presses, like humans, aren't quite perfect. Send us an email at ben@bclesterbooks.com with a photo of the misprint, and we will get another copy sent out to you!

WHO ARE B.C. LESTER BOOKS?

B.C. Lester Books is a small publishing firm of three people based in Buckinghamshire, UK. We aim to provide quality works in all things geography, for kids and adults, with varying interests. We have already released a selection of activity, trivia and fact books and are working hard to bring you wider selection. Have a suggestion for us? Then email ben@bclesterbooks.com. We are all ears!

HAVE FUN WITH OUR GIFT TO YOU: A 3-IN-1 GEOGRAPHY QUIZ BOOK!

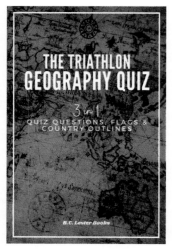

Go here to grab your FREE copy!
www.bclesterbooks.com/freebies/

EARTH FACTS & RECORDS

Earth Diameter: **12,742km^2(7919 miles)**
Circumference: **40,075km^2 (24,901 miles)**
Total Surface Area: **510,000,000km^2(196,940,000 sq mi)**
Land Surface Area: **148,326,000km^2(57,268,900 sq mi)** (29%)
Total World Population: **7,911,000,000**

Highest Mountain: **Mount Everest - 8848m** (Nepal/China)
Longest River: **River Nile − 6650km (4133 miles)** *(disputed)*
Largest Island: **Greenland − 2,160,000km^2(836,330 sq miles)**
Largest Lake: **Caspian Sea − 371,000km^2(146,000 sq miles)**
Largest City by Population: **Tokyo-Yokohama − 38,000,000 people** (Japan)
Tallest Waterfall: **Angel Falls − 979m** (Venezuela)
Deepest part of the Ocean: **Mariana Trench − 10,984m**
Hottest Temperature Recorded: **56.7°C/134.1F − Furnace Creek, USA** *(disputed)*
Coldest Temperature Recorded: **-89.2°C/-128.6F − Vostok Station, Antarctica**

CONTINENTS

NORTH AMERICA

EUROPE

ASIA

AFRICA

SOUTH AMERICA

AUSTRALIA & OCEANIA

ANTARCTICA

AFRICA
Number of Countries: **54** 1st ★
Area: **30,370,000 km^2(11,730,000 sq mi)** 2nd ★
Population: **1,340,598,000** 2nd ★
GDP: **$2.69T** 5th
Highest Point: **Mt. Kilimanjaro (5892m)** 4th

ANTARCTICA
Number of Countries: **0** 7th
Area: **14,200,000 km^2(5,500,000 sq mi)** 5th
Population: **1000** 7th
Highest Point: **Vinson Massif (4892m)** 6th

ASIA
Number of Countries: **48** 2nd ★
Area: **44,579,000 km^2(17,212,000 sq mi)** 1st ★
Population: **4,641,055,000** 1st ★
GDP: **$36.74T** 1st ★
Highest Point: **Mt. Everest (8848m)** 1st ★

AUSTRALIA & OCEANIA
Number of Countries: **14** 5th
Area: **8,526,000 km^2(3,292,000 sq mi)** 7th
Population: **42,678,000** 6th
GDP: **$1.89T** 6th
Highest Point: **Puncak Jaya (4884m)** 7th

EUROPE
Number of Countries: **46** 3rd ★
Area: **10,180,000 km^2 (3,930,000 sq mi)** 5th
Population: **747,636,000** 3rd ★
GDP: **$23.50T** 3rd ★
Highest Point: **Mt. Elbrus (5642m)** 5th

NORTH AMERICA
Number of Countries: **23** 4th
Area: **24,709,000 km^2(9,540,000 sq mi)** 3rd ★
Population: **579,072,000** 4th
GDP: **$26.80T** 2nd ★
Highest Point: **Denali (6191m)** 3rd ★

SOUTH AMERICA
Number of Countries: **12** 6th
Area: **17,840,000 km^2(6,890,000 sq mi)** 4th
Population: **430,760,000** 5th
GDP: **$3.24T** 4th
Highest Point: **Aconcagua (6962m)** 2nd ★

WORLD MAP

* the flag of the Islamic Emirate is also used.

AFGHANISTAN افغانستان
ASIA ◖
Capital: **Kabul**
Area: **652,230 km² (251,830 sq mi)** 40th
Population: **38,928,000** 42nd
GDP: **$19.9B** 117th   Currency: **Afghani (AFN)**
Highest Point: **Noshaq (7492m)** 6th
Official Languages: **Dari/Pashto**

ALBANIA SHQIPËRIA
EUROPE ◖
Capital: **Tirana**
Area: **28,748 km² (11,100 sq mi)** 140th
Population: **2,878,000** 135th
GDP: **$17.1B** 125th   Currency: **Lek (ALL)**
Highest Point: **Mt. Korab (2764m)** 78th
Official Languages: **Albanian**

ALGERIA الجزائر
AFRICA ◖
Capital: **Algiers**
Area: **2,381,741 km² (919,595 sq mi)** 10th
Population: **43,851,000** 32nd
GDP: **$151B** 58th   Currency: **Dinar (DZD)**
Highest Point: **Mt.Tahat (3003m)** 61st
Official Languages: **Arabic/Berber**

ANDORRA ANDORRA
EUROPE ⊞
Capital: **Andorra La Vella**
Area: **468 km² (181 sq mi)** 180th
Population: **77,000** 186th
GDP: **$3.24B** 154th   Currency: **Euro (EUR)**
Highest Point: **Coma Pedrosa (2942m)** 68th
Official Languages: **Catalan**

1804	1810	1813		1901	1912	1919		1962	1975	1981	1991
10	7	4		9	2	1		3	5	6	11 · 8

SOVEREIGNTY BY COUNTRY
● =Independence, ● =Formed

ANGOLA ANGOLA
AFRICA
Capital: **Luanda**
Area: **1,246,700km²** **(481,400 sq mi)** 22nd
Population: **32,866,000** 45th
GDP: **$66.5B** 75th   Currency: **Kwanza (AOA)**
Highest Point: **Morro De Moco (2620m)** 87th
Official Languages: **Portuguese**

ANTIGUA & BARBUDA
N. AMERICA   ANTIGUA & BARBUDA
Capital: **St. Johns**
Area: **440km²** **(170 sq mi)** 183rd
Population: **98,000** 185th
GDP: **$1.38B** 179th   Currency: **Dollar (XCD)**
Highest Point: **Mt. Obama (402m)** 170th
Official Languages: **English**

ARGENTINA ARGENTINA
S. AMERICA
Capital: **Buenos Aires**
Area: **2,780,400km²** **(1,073,500 sq mi)** 8th
Population: **45,195,000** 31st
GDP: **$418B** 32ND   Currency: **Peso (ARS)**
Highest Point: **Aconcagua (6962m)** 9th
Official Languages: **(Spanish)**

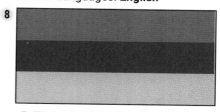

ARMENIA Հայաստան
ASIA
Capital: **Yerevan**
Area: **29,743km²** **(11,484 sq mi)** 138th
Population: **2,963,000** 134th
GDP: **$12.3B** 139th   Currency: **Dram (AMD)**
Highest Point: **Mt. Aragats (4049m)** 39th
Official Languages: **Armenian**

AUSTRALIA AUSTRALIA
AUS. & OCEANIA
Capital: **Canberra**
Area: **7,692,024 km²** **(2,969,907 sq mi)** 6th
Population: **25,500,000** 53rd
GDP: **$1.62T** 12th   Currency: **Dollar (AUD)**
Highest Point: **Mt. Kosciuszko (2620m)** 107th
Official Languages: **English**

AUSTRIA ÖSTERREICH
EUROPE
Capital: **Vienna**
Area: **83,879 km²** **(32,386 sq mi)** 113rd
Population: **9,006,000** 98th
GDP: **$482B** 28th   Currency: **Euro (EUR)**
Highest Point: **Grobglockner (3798m)** 42nd
Official Languages: **German**

AZERBAIJAN
ASIA   AZƏRBAYCAN
Capital: **Baku**
Area: **86,600km²** **(33,400 sq mi)** 112nd
Population: **10,139,000** 90th
GDP: **$49.9B** 89th   Currency: **Manat (AZN)**
Highest Point: **Mt. Bazarduzu (4466m)** 34th
Official Languages: **Azerbaijani**

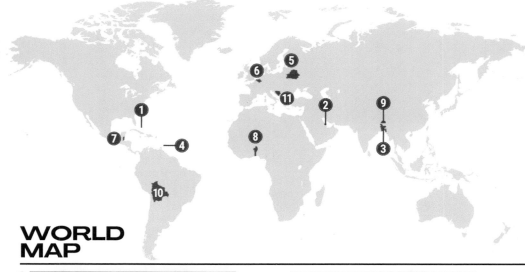

WORLD MAP

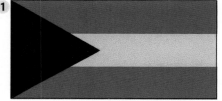

BAHAMAS, THE BAHAMAS, THE
N. AMERICA 🇧🇸
Capital: **Nassau**
Area: **13,878km² (5358 sq mi)** 155th
Population: **393,000** 171st
GDP: **$11.7B** 144th   Currency: **Dollar (BSD)**
Highest Point: **Mt. Alvernia (63m)** 189th
Official Languages: **English**

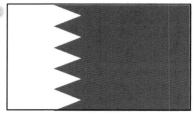

BAHRAIN البحرين
ASIA ☪
Capital: **Manama**
Area: **778 km² (301 sq mi)** 174th
Population: **1,702,000** 150th
GDP: **$37.5B** 99th   Currency: **Dinar (BHD)**
Highest Point: **Mountain of Smoke (134m)** 183rd
Official Languages: **Arabic**

BANGLADESH
ASIA ☪   বাংলাদেশ
Capital: **Dhaka**
Area: **147,050km² (56,980 sq mi)** 92nd
Population: **164,889,000** 8th
GDP: **$410B** 33rd   Currency: **Taka (BDT)**
Highest Point: **Keokradong (1064m)** 145th
Official Languages: **Bengali**

BARBADOS BARBADOS
N. AMERICA 🇧🇧
Capital: **Bridgetown**
Area: **439km² (169 sq mi)** 184th
Population: **287,000** 175th
GDP: **$4.63B** 156th   Currency: **Dollar (BBD)**
Highest Point: **Mt. Hillaby (340m)** 172nd
Official Languages: **English**

1634   1825 1830   1960 1966 1971 1973   1981   1991 1992

 9   10 6   8 4 2 1 1   7   5 11

SOVEREIGNTY BY COUNTRY
 =Independence, =Formed

5

BELARUS Беларусь
EUROPE
Capital: **Minsk**
Area: **207,595km² (80,153 sq mi)** 84th
Population: **9,449,000** 93rd
GDP: **$60.7B** 81st   Currency: **Ruble (BYN)**
Highest Point: **Dzyarzhynsk Hill (345m)** 171st
Official Languages: **Belarusian/Russian**

6

BELGIUM BELGIË/BELGIQUE
EUROPE
Capital: **Brussels**
Area: **30,688 km² (11,849 sq mi)** 136th
Population: **11,589,000** 81st
GDP: **$579B** 25th   Currency: **Euro (EUR)**
Highest Point: **Signal De Botrange (694m)** 164th
Official Languages: **Dutch/French/German**

7

BELIZE BELIZE
N. AMERICA
Capital: **Belmopan**
Area: **22,966 km² (8867 sq mi)** 147th
Population: **398,000** 170th
GDP: **$1.70B** 175th   Currency: **Dollar (BZD)**
Highest Point: **Doyle's Delight (1124m)** 143rd
Official Languages: **English**

8

BENIN BÉNIN
AFRICA
Capital: **Porto-Novo**
Area: **114,763 km² (44,310 sq mi)** 100th
Population: **12,123,000** 77th
GDP: **$17.3B** 124th   Currency: **Franc (XOF)**
Highest Point: **Mt. Sokbaro (658m)** 165th
Official Languages: **French**

9

BHUTAN འབྲུག་ཡུལ
ASIA
Capital: **Thimphu**
Area: **38,394km² (14,824 sq mi)** 133rd
Population: **772,000** 162nd
GDP: **$2.48B** 167th   Currency: **Ngultrum (BTN)**
Highest Point: **Gangkhar Puensum (7570m)** 4th
Official Languages: **Dzongkha**

10

BOLIVIA BOLIVIA
S. AMERICA
Capital: **La Paz**
Area: **1,098,581 km² (424,164 sq mi)** 27th
Population: **11,673,000** 80th
GDP: **$43.1B** 93rd   Currency: **Boliviano (BOB)**
Highest Point: **Nevado Sajama (6542m)** 12th
Official Languages: **Spanish (+36 others)**

11

BOSNIA & HERZEGOVINA
EUROPE   BOSNA I HERCEGOVINA
Capital: **Sarajevo**
Area: **51,129km² (19,741 sq mi)** 125th
Population: **3,281,000** 133rd
GDP: **$22.0B** 115th   Currency: **Mark (BAM)**
Highest Point: **Maglic (2386m)** 100th
Official Languages: **(Bosnian/Serbian/Croatian)**

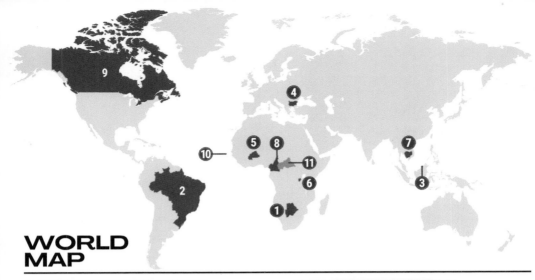

WORLD MAP

BOTSWANA BOTSWANA
AFRICA

Capital: **Gaborone**
Area: **581,730km^2 (224,610 sq mi)** 47th
Population: **2,352,000** 142nd
GDP: **$18.7B** 122nd   Currency: **Pula (BWP)**
Highest Point: **Monalanong Hill (1494m)** 131st
Official Languages: **English/Setswana**

BRAZIL BRASIL
S. AMERICA

Capital: **Brasilia**
Area: **8,515,767km^2 (3,287,956 sq mi)** 5th
Population: **212,519,000** 6th
GDP: **$1.49T** 13th   Currency: **Real (BRR)**
Highest Point: **Pico de Neblina (2994m)** 64th
Official Languages: **Portuguese**

BRUNEI BRUNEI
ASIA

Capital: **Bandar Seri Begawan**
Area: **5765 km^2 (2226 sq mi)** 165th
Population: **437,000** 169th
GDP: **$15.3B** 131st   Currency: **Dollar (BND)**
Highest Point: **Bukit Pagon (1850m)** 125th
Official Languages: **Malay**

BULGARIA Болгария
EUROPE

Capital: **Sofia**
Area: **110,994 km^2 (42,855 sq mi)** 103rd
Population: **6,948,000** 104th
GDP: **$77.8B** 70th   Currency: **Lev (BGN)**
Highest Point: **Musala (2925m)** 69th
Official Languages: **Bulgarian**

1822		1867		1908		1953	1960	1961	1962	1966		1975	1984
2		9		4		7	11 5 8 6			1		10	3

SOVEREIGNTY BY COUNTRY
●=Independence,   ●=Formed

BURKINA FASO
AFRICA 🇨 BURKINA FASO
Capital: **Ouagadougou**
Area: **274,200km² (105,900 sq mi)** 74th
Population: **20,903,000** 58th
GDP: **$18.9B** 121st Currency: **Franc (XOF)**
Highest Point: **Tenakourou (749m)** 163rd
Official Languages: **French**

BURUNDI BURUNDI
AFRICA 🇧🇮
Capital: **Gitega**
Area: **27,834km² (10,747 sq mi)** 142nd
Population: **11,891,000** 82nd
GDP: **$3.24B** 164th Currency: **Franc (BIF)**
Highest Point: **Mt. Heha (2685m)** 82nd
Official Languages: **English/French/Kirundi**

CAMBODIA កម្ពុជា
ASIA 🌐
Capital: **Phnom Penh**
Area: **181,035 km² (69,898 sq mi)** 88th
Population: **16,719,000** 73rd
GDP: **$27.2B** 104th Currency: **Riel (KHR)**
Highest Point: **Phnom Aural (1813m)** 127th
Official Languages: **Khmer**

CAMEROON CAMEROON
AFRICA 🇨🇲
Capital: **Yaounde**
Area: **475,442km² (183,569 sq mi)** 53rd
Population: **26,546,000** 55th
GDP: **$44.9B** 91st Currency: **Franc (XAF)**
Highest Point: **Mt. Cameroon (4095m)** 40th
Official Languages: **English/French**

CANADA CANADA
N. AMERICA 🇨🇦
Capital: **Ottawa**
Area: **9,984,670km² (3,855,100 sq mi)** 2nd ★
Population: **37,742,000** 38th
GDP: **$1.88T** 9th Currency: **Dollar (CAD)**
Highest Point: **Mt. Logan (5959m)** 15th
Official Languages: **English/French**

CAPE VERDE CABO VERDE
AFRICA 🇨🇻
Capital: **Praia**
Area: **4033km² (1557 sq mi)** 167th
Population: **556,000** 167th
GDP: **$2.00B** 172nd Currency: **Escudo (CVE)**
Highest Point: **Mt. Fogo (2829m)** 74th
Official Languages: **Portuguese**

CENTRAL AFRICAN REPUBLIC
AFRICA 🇨🇫 KÖDÖRÖSÊSE TÎ BÊAFRÎKA
Capital: **Bangui**
Area: **622,984 km² (240,535 sq mi)** 44th
Population: **4,830,000** 114th
GDP: **$2.72B** 165th Currency: **Franc (XAF)**
Highest Point: **Mt. Ngaoui (1420m)** 134th
Official Languages: **French/Sango**

9

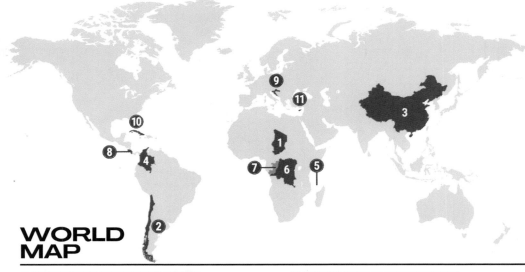

WORLD MAP

CHAD TCHAD/تشاد
AFRICA
Capital: **N'Djenma**
Area: **1,284,000km^2 (496,000 sq mi)** 20th
Population: **16,426,000** 70th
GDP: **$12.5B** 137th   Currency: **Franc (XAF)**
Highest Point: **Emi Koussi (3445m)** 51st
Official Languages: **French/Arabic**

CHILE CHILE
S. AMERICA
Capital: **Santiago**
Area: **756,096km^2 (291,930 sq mi)** 37th
Population: **19,116,000** 60th
GDP: **$308B** 43rd   Currency: **Peso (CLP)**
Highest Point: **Ojos del Salado (6893m)** 10th
Official Languages: **(Spanish)**

CHINA 中国
ASIA
Capital: **Beijing**
Area: **9,596,961km^2 (3,705,407 sq mi)** 4th
Population: **1,439,323,000** 1st ★
GDP: **$16.6T** 2nd ★   Currency: **Yuan (CNY)**
Highest Point: **Mt. Everest (8848m)** 1st ★
Official Languages: **Standard Chinese**

COLOMBIA COLOMBIA
S. AMERICA
Capital: **Bogota**
Area: **1,141,748km^2 (440,831 sq mi)** 25th
Population: **50,883,000** 28th
GDP: **$296B** 45th   Currency: **Peso (COP)**
Highest Point: **Pico Cristobal Colon (5700m)** 18th
Official Languages: **Spanish**

SOVEREIGNTY BY COUNTRY
●=Independence, ●=Formed

COMOROS KOMORI
AFRICA
Capital: **Moroni**
Area: **1,659km² (641 sq mi)** 171st
Population: **870,000** 161st
GDP: **$1.31B** 180th   Currency: **Franc (KMF)**
Highest Point: **Mt. Karthala (2360m)** 101st
Official Languages: **Arabic/Comorian/French**

CONGO, D. R. OF THE
AFRICA   REP. DEM. DU CONGO
Capital: **Kinshasa**
Area: **2,345,409km² (905,567 sq mi)** 11th
Population: **89,561,000** 16th
GDP: **$55.1B** 87th   Currency: **Franc (CDF)**
Highest Point: **Mt. Stanley (5109m)** 25th
Official Languages: **French**

CONGO, REPUBLIC OF THE
AFRICA   REPUBLIQUE DU CONGO
Capital: **Brazzaville**
Area: **342,000km² (132,000 sq mi)** 64th
Population: **5,518,000** 115th
GDP: **$12.0B** 141st   Currency: **Franc (XAF)**
Highest Point: **Mt. Nabeba (1020m)** 149th
Official Languages: **French**

COSTA RICA COSTA RICA
N. AMERICA
Capital: **San Jose**
Area: **51,100km² (19,700 sq mi)** 126th
Population: **5,094,000** 119th
GDP: **$61.2B** 80th   Currency: **Colon (CRC)**
Highest Point: **Cerro Chirripo (3820m)** 41st
Official Languages: **Spanish**

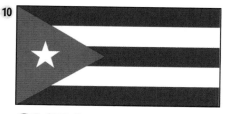

CROATIA HRVATSKA
EUROPE
Capital: **Zagreb**
Area: **56,594km² (21,851 sq mi)** 124th
Population: **4,105,000** 128th
GDP: **$65.2B** 77th   Currency: **Kuna (HRK)**
Highest Point: **Dinara (1831m)** 126th
Official Languages: **Croatian**

CUBA CUBA
N. AMERICA
Capital: **Havana**
Area: **109,884km² (42,426 sq mi)** 104th
Population: **11,327,000** 83rd
GDP: **$101B** 63rd   Currency: **Peso (CUP)**
Highest Point: **Pico Turquino (1974m)** 116th
Official Languages: **Spanish**

CYPRUS ΚΥΠΡΟΣ/KIBRIS
EUROPE
Capital: **Nicosia**
Area: **9251km² (3572 sq mi)** 163rd
Population: **1,207,000** 159th
GDP: **$26.5B** 105th   Currency: **Euro (EUR)**
Highest Point: **Mt. Olympus (1951m)** 117th
Official Languages: **Greek/Turkish**

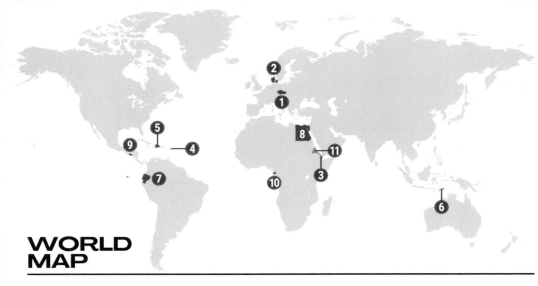

WORLD MAP

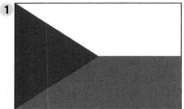

CZECH REPUBLIC
EUROPE 🏳

Capital: **Prague**
Area: **78,866 km² (30,450 sq mi)** 115th
Population: **10,709,000** 86th
GDP: **$276B** 48th   Currency: **Koruna (CZK)**
Highest Point: **Snezka (1603m)** 129th
Official Languages: **Czech**

DENMARK DANMARK
EUROPE 🏳

Capital: **Copenhagen**
Area*: **42,933km² (16,339 sq mi)** 130th
Population*: **5,792,000** 112th
GDP*: **$393B** 37th   Currency: **Krone (DKK)**
Highest Point*: **Mollehoj (171m)** 180th
Official Languages: **Danish**
*excluding Faroe Islands and Greenland

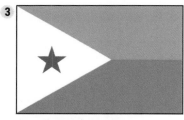

DJIBOUTI DJIBOUTI/جيبوتي
AFRICA ☪

Capital: **Djibouti City**
Area: **23,200km² (9000 sq mi)** 146th
Population: **988,000** 156th
GDP: **$3.66B** 162nd   Currency: **Franc (DJF)**
Highest Point: **Mousa Ali (2028m)** 113th
Official Languages: **French/Arabic**

DOMINICA DOMINICA
N. AMERICA 🏳

Capital: **Roseau**
Area: **750km² (290 sq mi)** 175th
Population: **72,000** 187th
GDP: **$523M** 187th   Currency: **Dollar (XCD)**
Highest Point: **Morne Diablotins (1447m)** 132nd
Official Languages: **English**

714	1821	1822	1844	1922	1968	1977	1978	1993	2002
2	9	7	5	8	10	3	4	11 1	6

SOVEREIGNTY BY COUNTRY
● =Independence, ● =Formed

DOMINICAN REP.
N. AMERICA ⚑ REP. DOMINICANA
Capital: **Santo Domingo**
Area: **48,671 km² (18,792 sq mi)** 128th
Population: **10,848,000** 87th
GDP: **$83.9B** 68th
Highest Point: **Pico Duarte (3098m)** 55th
Official Languages: **Spanish**
Currency: **Peso (DOP)**

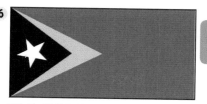

EAST TIMOR TIMOR-LESTE
ASIA ⚑
Capital: **Dili**
Area: **15,007km² (5794 sq mi)** 154th
Population: **1,318,000** 154th
GDP: **$1.73B** 174th Currency: **Dollar (USD)**
Highest Point: **Mt. Ramelau (2963m)** 65th
Official Languages: **Portuguese/Tetum**

ECUADOR ECUADOR
S. AMERICA ⚑
Capital: **Quito**
Area: **283,561km² (109,484 sq mi)** 73rd
Population: **17,643,000** 65th
GDP: **$100B** 64th Currency: **Dollar (USD)**
Highest Point: **Chimborazo (6267m)** 13th
Official Languages: **Spanish**

EGYPT مصر
AFRICA ☪
Capital: **Cairo**
Area: **1,010,408km² (390,121 sq mi)** 29th
Population: **102,334,000** 13th
GDP: **$394B** 36th Currency: **Pound (EGP)**
Highest Point: **Mt. Catherine (2629m)** 86th
Official Languages: **Arabic**

EL SALVADOR EL SALVADOR
N. AMERICA ⚑
Capital: **San Salvador**
Area: **21,041 km² (8124 sq mi)** 148th
Population: **6,486,000** 108th
GDP: **$26.3B** 106th Currency: **Dollar (USD), Bitcoin (BTC)**
Highest Point: **Cerro El Pital (2730m)** 81st
Official Languages: **Spanish**

EQUATORIAL GUINEA
AFRICA ⚑ GUINEA ECUATORIAL
Capital: **Malabo**
Area: **28,050km² (10,830 sq mi)** 141st
Population: **1,403,000** 151th
GDP: **$11.7B** 143rd Currency: **Franc (XAF)**
Highest Point: **Pico Basile (3008m)** 60th
Official Languages: **French/Portuguese/Spanish**

ERITREA ERITREA/إرتريا
AFRICA ⚑☪
Capital: **Asmara**
Area: **117,600km² (45,400 sq mi)** 99th
Population: **3,546,000** 130th
GDP: **$2.25B** 170th Currency: **Nakfa (ERN)**
Highest Point: **Embe Soira (3018m)** 58th
Official Languages: **(Arabic/English/Tigrinya)**

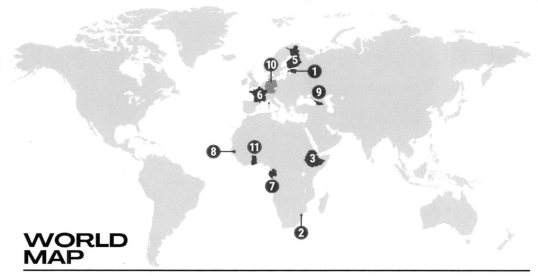

WORLD MAP

ESTONIA EESTI
EUROPE ◙
Capital: **Tallinn**
Area: **45,227km² (17,462 sq mi)** 129th
Population: **1,327,000** 153rd
GDP: **$35.2B** 102nd   Currency: **Euro (EUR)**
Highest Point: **Suur Mugamani (318m)** 173rd
Official Languages: **Estonian**

ESWATINI ESWATINI
AFRICA ⛉
Capital: **Mbabane**
Area: **17,364 km² (6704 sq mi)** 153rd
Population: **1,160,000** 157th
GDP: **$4.23B** 161st   Currency: **Lilangeni (SZL)**
Highest Point: **Emlembe (1862m)** 122nd
Official Languages: **English/Swazi**

ETHIOPIA ኢትዮጵያ
AFRICA ⛉
Capital: **Addis Ababa**
Area: **1,104,300km² (426,400 sq mi)** 26th
Population: **114,964,000** 14th
GDP: **$94.0B** 65th   Currency: **Birr (ETB)**
Highest Point: **Ras Dejen (4550m)** 31st
Official Languages: **Amharic**

FIJI VITI/फ़िजी
AUS & OCEANIA ⛉
Capital: **Suva**
Area: **18,274km² (7056 sq mi)** 151st
Population: **896,000** 158th
GDP: **$4.59B** 157th   Currency: **Dollar (FJD)**
Highest Point: **Tomanivi (1324m)** 136th
Official Languages: **English/Fijian/Fiji Hindi**

100 481 843   1918   1953   1960   1965 1968 1970   1991

3 6 10   5   11   7   8 2 4   9

SOVEREIGNTY BY COUNTRY
● =Independence, ● =Formed

FINLAND SUOMI/FINLAND
EUROPE
Capital: **Helsinki**
Area: **338,424km² (130,666 sq mi)** 65th
Population: **5,541,000** 116th
GDP: **$300B** 44th Currency: **Euro (EUR)**
Highest Point: **Halti (1324m)** 137th
Official Languages: **Finnish/Swedish**

FRANCE FRANCE
EUROPE
Capital: **Paris**
Area: **640,679km² (247,368 sq mi)** 42nd
Population: **65,274,000** 20th
GDP: **$2.94T** 7th Currency: **Euro(EUR)**
Highest Point: **Mont Blanc (4808m)** 28th
Official Languages: **French**

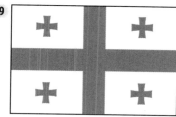

GABON GABON
AFRICA
Capital: **Libreville**
Area: **267,667km² (103,347 sq mi)** 76th
Population: **2,226,000** 143rd
GDP: **$18.3B** 123rd Currency: **Franc (XAF)**
Highest Point: **Mont Bengoue (1070m)** 144th
Official Languages: **French**

GAMBIA, THE THE GAMBIA
AFRICA
Capital: **Bangul**
Area: **10,689km² (4127 sq mi)** 159th
Population: **2,417,000** 141st
GDP: **$2.08B** 171st Currency: **Dalasi (GMD)**
Highest Point: **Red Rock (53m)** 188th
Official Languages: **English**

GEORGIA საქართველო
ASIA
Capital: **Tbilisi**
Area: **69,700m² (26,900 sq mi)** 119th
Population: **3,989,000** 129th
GDP: **$16.2B** 129th Currency: **Lari (GEL)**
Highest Point: **Shkhara (5201m)** 22nd
Official Languages: **Georgian/Abkhazian**

GERMANY DEUTSCHLAND
EUROPE
Capital: **Berlin**
Area: **357,386 km² (137,988 sq mi)** 63rd
Population: **83,784,000** 18th
GDP: **$4.32T** 4th Currency: **Euro (EUR)**
Highest Point: **Zugspitze (2962m)** 66th
Official Languages: **German**

GHANA GHANA
AFRICA
Capital: **Accra**
Area: **239,567km² (92,497 sq mi)** 80th
Population: **31,073,000** 46th
GDP: **$74.3B** 72nd Currency: **Cedi (GHS)**
Highest Point: **Mt. Afadjato (880m)** 157th
Official Languages: **English**

15

WORLD MAP

1

GREECE ΕΛΛΆΔΑ
EUROPE

Capital: **Athens**
Area: **131,957km² (50,949 sq mi)** 95th
Population: **10,423,000** 85th
GDP: **$210B** 52nd   Currency: **Euro (EUR)**
Highest Point: **Mt. Olympus (2919m)** 70th
Official Languages: **Greek**

2

GRENADA GRENADA
N. AMERICA

Capital: **St George's**
Area: **349km² (135 sq mi)** 186th
Population: **113,000** 180th
GDP: **$1.04B** 181st   Currency: **Dollar (XCD)**
Highest Point: **Mt. Saint Catherine (840m)** 159th
Official Languages: **English**

3

GUATEMALA GUATEMALA
N. AMERICA

Capital: **Guatemala City**
Area: **108,889 km² (42,042 sq mi)** 105th
Population: **17,916,000** 68th
GDP: **$81.4B** 69th   Currency: **Quetzal (GTQ)**
Highest Point: **Volcan Tajumulco (4220m)** 36th
Official Languages: **Spanish**

4

GUINEA GUINÉE
AFRICA

Capital: **Conakry**
Area: **245,836km² (94,918 sq mi)** 77th
Population: **13,132,000** 76th
GDP: **$16.3B** 128th   Currency: **Franc (GNF)**
Highest Point: **Mont Nimba (1752m)** 128th
Official Languages: **French**

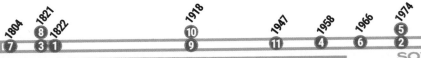

SOVEREIGNTY BY COUNTRY
●=Independence, ●=Formed

GUINEA-BISSAU
AFRICA ◖ GUINÉ-BISSAU

Capital: **Bissau**
Area: **36,125km² (13,948 sq mi)** 40th
Population: **1,968,000** 149th
GDP: **$1.65B** 177th Currency: **Franc (XOF)**
Highest Point: **Unnamed (300m)** 176th
Official Languages: **Portuguese**

GUYANA GUYANA
S. AMERICA ⬝

Capital: **Georgetown**
Area: **214,970km² (83,000 sq mi)** 83rd
Population: **787,000** 159th
GDP: **$7.26B** 153rd Currency: **Dollar (GYD)**
Highest Point: **Mt. Roraima (2772m)** 77th
Official Languages: **English**

HAITI HAÏTI
N. AMERICA ⬝

Capital: **Port-Au-Prince**
Area: **27,750 km² (10,710 sq mi)** 143rd
Population: **11,403,000** 78th
GDP: **$22.4B** 113rd Currency: **Gourde (HTG)**
Highest Point: **Pic La Selle (2680m)** 83rd
Official Languages: **French/Haitian Creole**

HONDURAS HONDURAS
N. AMERICA ⬝

Capital: **Tegucigalpa**
Area: **112,492 km² (43,433 sq mi)** 101st
Population: **9,905,000** 95th
GDP: **$26.2B** 107th Currency: **Lempira (HNL)**
Highest Point: **Cerros La Minas (2870m)** 72nd
Official Languages: **Spanish**

HUNGARY MAGYARORSZÁG
EUROPE ⬝

Capital: **Budapest**
Area: **93,030km² (35,920 sq mi)** 108th
Population: **9,660,000** 92nd
GDP: **$176B** 55th Currency: **Forint (HUF)**
Highest Point: **Kekes (1014m)** 150th
Official Languages: **Hungarian**

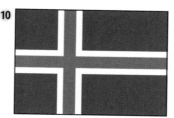

ICELAND ÍSLAND
EUROPE ⬝

Capital: **Reykjavik**
Area: **102,775km² (39,682 sq mi)** 106th
Population: **341,000** 173rd
GDP: **$24.2B** 112th Currency: **Krona (ISK)**
Highest Point: **Hvannadalshknukur (2110m)** 109th
Official Languages: **Icelandic**

INDIA BHĀRAT
ASIA ▦

Capital: **New Delhi**
Area: **3,287,263 km² (1,269,219 sq mi)** 6th
Population: **1,380,004,000** 2nd ★
GDP: **$3.05T** 6th Currency: **Rupee (INR)**
Highest Point: **Kangchenjunga (8586m)** 3rd ★
Official Languages: **English/Hindi**

17

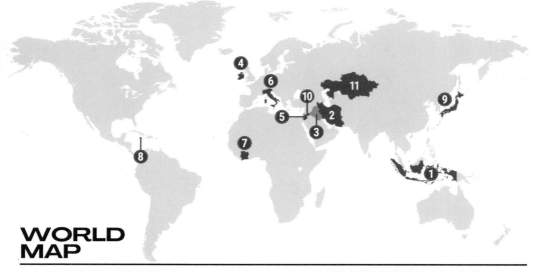

WORLD MAP

INDONESIA INDONESIA
ASIA C
Capital: **Jakarta**
Area: **1,904,569 km² (735,358 sq mi)** 14th
Population: **273,524,000** 4th
GDP: **$1.16T** 16th   Currency: **Rupiah (IDR)**
Highest Point: **Puncak Jaya (4884m)** 27th
Official Languages: **Indonesian**

IRAN ایران
ASIA C
Capital: **Tehran**
Area: **1,648,195 km² (636,372 sq mi)** 17th
Population: **83,993,000** 17th
GDP: **$683B** 22nd   Currency: **Rial (ALL)**
Highest Point: **Mt. Davamand (5610m)** 21st
Official Languages: **Persian**

IRAQ عێراق/ٱلْعِرَاق
ASIA C
Capital: **Baghdad**
Area: **437,072km² (168,754 sq mi)** 58th
Population: **40,222,000** 36th
GDP: **$191B** 53rd   Currency: **Dinar (IQD)**
Highest Point: **Cheekha Dar (3611m)** 47th
Official Languages: **Arabic/Kurdish**

IRELAND IRELAND/ÉIRE
EUROPE ⵀ
Capital: **Dublin**
Area: **70,723 km² (27,133 sq mi)** 118th
Population: **4,938,000** 121st
GDP: **$477B** 29th   Currency: **Euro (EUR)**
Highest Point: **Carrauntoohil (1038m)** 146th
Official Languages: **English/Irish**

SOVEREIGNTY BY COUNTRY
● =Independence,   ● =Formed

5

ISRAEL ישראל
ASIA 🔲
Capital: **Jerusalem**
Area: **20,770km² (8019 sq mi)** 149th
Population: **8,656,000** 96th
GDP: **$447B** 30th Currency: **Shekel (ILS)**
Highest Point: **Mt. Meron (1208m)** 140th
Official Languages: **Hebrew**

6

ITALY ITALIA
EUROPE 🎏
Capital: **Rome**
Area: **301,340km² (116,350 sq mi)** 71st
Population: **60,462,000** 23rd
GDP: **$2.11T** 8th Currency: **Euro (EUR)**
Highest Point: **Mt. Blanc (4808m)** 28th
Official Languages: **Italian**

7

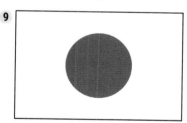

IVORY COAST CÔTE D'IVOIRE
AFRICA 🎏🎏
Capital: **Yamoussoukro/Abidjan**
Area: **322,463 km² (124,504 sq mi)** 68th
Population: **26,378,000** 51st
GDP: **$71.0B** 74th Currency: **Franc (XOF)**
Highest Point: **Mont Nimba (1752m)** 128th
Official Languages: **French**

8

JAMAICA JAMAICA
N. AMERICA 🎏
Capital: **Kingston**
Area: **10,991 km² (4244 sq mi)** 160th
Population: **2,961,000** 138th
GDP: **$14.6B** 133rd Currency: **Dollar (JMD)**
Highest Point: **Blue Mountain Peak (2256m)** 106th
Official Languages: **English**

9

JAPAN 日本
ASIA 🎏FOLK
Capital: **Tokyo**
Area: **377,973km² (145,936 sq mi)** 62nd
Population: **126,476,000** 11th
GDP: **$5.38T** 3rd ★ Currency: **Yen (JPY)**
Highest Point: **Mt. Fuji (3776m)** 43rd
Official Languages: **(Japanese)**

10

JORDAN الأردن
ASIA 🎏
Capital: **Amman**
Area: **89,342km² (34,495 sq mi)** 110th
Population: **10,203,000** 84th
GDP: **$45.0B** 90th Currency: **Dinar (JOD)**
Highest Point: **Jabal Umm ad Dami (1854m)** 124th
Official Languages: **Arabic**

11

KAZAKHSTAN ҚАЗАҚСТАН
ASIA 🎏
Capital: **Nur-Sultan**
Area: **2,724,900km² (1,052,100 sq mi)** 9th
Population: **18,776,000** 63rd
GDP: **$188B** 54th Currency: **Tenge (KZT)**
Highest Point: **Khan Tengri (7010m)** 8th
Official Languages: **Kazakh/Russian**

WORLD MAP

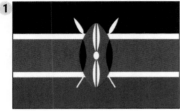

KENYA KENYA
AFRICA ⚑
Capital: **Nairobi**
Area: **580,367 km² (224,081 sq mi)** 47th
Population: **53,771,000** 29th
GDP: **$106B** 62nd   Currency: **Shilling (KES)**
Highest Point: **Mt. Kenya (5199m)** 23rd
Official Languages: **English/Swahili**

KIRIBATI KIRIBATI
AUS & OCEANIA ⚑
Capital: **Tarawa**
Area: **811km² (313 sq mi)** 173rd
Population: **119,000** 179th
GDP: **$231M** 192nd   Currency: **Dollar (AUD)**
Highest Point: **Unnamed (81m)** 185th
Official Languages: **English/Gilbertese**

KOREA, NORTH 조선
ASIA ◎
Capital: **Pyongyang**
Area: **120,540km² (46,540 sq mi)** 97th
Population: **25,779,000** 54th
GDP: **$30.0B** 103rd   Currency: **Won (KPW)**
Highest Point: **Paektu-San (2744m)** 80th
Official Languages: **Korean**

KOREA, SOUTH 한국
ASIA ◎
Capital: **Seoul**
Area: **100,363km² (38,750 sq mi)** 107th
Population: **51,269,000** 27th
GDP: **$1.81T** 10th   Currency: **Won (KRW)**
Highest Point: **Halla-San (1950m)** 118th
Official Languages: **Korean**

SOVEREIGNTY BY COUNTRY
 =Independence, =Formed

5

KOSOVO KOSOVË/KOCOBO
EUROPE
Capital: **Pristina**
Area: **10,887 km² (4230 sq mi)** 161st
Population: **1,782,000** 148th
GDP: **$7.84B** 149th Currency: **Euro (EUR)**
Highest Point: **Velika Rudoka (2658m)** 84th
Official Languages: **Albanian/Serbian**

6

KUWAIT الكويت
ASIA
Capital: **Kuwait City**
Area: **17,818 km² (6880 sq mi)** 152th
Population: **4,271,000** 125th
GDP: **$127B** 59th Currency: **Dinar (KWD)**
Highest Point: **Multa Ridge (306m)** 175th
Official Languages: **Arabic**

7

KYRGYZSTAN
ASIA Кыргызстан
Capital: **Bishkek**
Area: **199,951km² (77,202 sq mi)** 85th
Population: **6,524,000** 109th
GDP: **$7.47B** 152nd Currency: **Som (KGS)**
Highest Point: **Jengish Chokusu (7439m)** 7th
Official Languages: **Kyrgyz/Russian**

8

LAOS ລາວ
ASIA
Capital: **Vientiane**
Area: **237,955km² (91,875 sq mi)** 82nd
Population: **7,276,000** 103rd
GDP: **$20.4B** 116th Currency: **Kip (LAK)**
Highest Point: **Phou Bia (2817m)** 75th
Official Languages: **Lao**

9

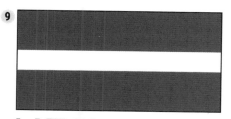

LATVIA LATVIJA
EUROPE
Capital: **Riga**
Area: **64,589km² (24,938 sq mi)** 122nd
Population: **1,886,000** 147th
GDP: **$37.7B** 98th Currency: **Euro (EUR)**
Highest Point: **Gaizinkalns (312m)** 174th
Official Languages: **Latvian**

10

LEBANON لبنان
ASIA
Capital: **Beirut**
Area: **10,452 km² (4036 sq mi)** 162nd
Population: **6,825,000** 107th
GDP: **$19.1B** 119th Currency: **Pound (LBP)**
Highest Point: **Qurnat as Sawda' (3088m)** 56th
Official Languages: **Arabic**

11

LESOTHO LESOTHO
AFRICA
Capital: **Maseru**
Area: **30,355 km² (11,720 sq mi)** 137th
Population: **2,142,000** 146th
GDP: **$2.46B** 169th Currency: **Loti (LSL)**
Highest Point: **Thabana Ntlenyana (3482m)** 48th
Official Languages: **English/Sesotho**

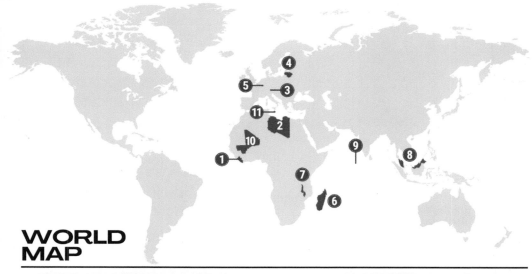

WORLD MAP

LIBERIA LIBERIA
AFRICA
Capital: **Monrovia**
Area: **111,369 km² (43,000 sq mi)** 113rd
Population: **5,058,000** 123rd
GDP: **$3.37B** 163rd   Currency: **Dollar (LRD)**
Highest Point: **Mt. Wuteve (1440m)** 133rd
Official Languages: **English**

LIBYA ليبيا
AFRICA
Capital: **Tripoli**
Area: **1,759,541km² (679,363 sq mi)** 16th
Population: **6,871,000** 106th
GDP: **$24.3B** 111th   Currency: **Dinar (LYD)**
Highest Point: **Bikku Bitti (2267m)** 105th
Official Languages: **Arabic**

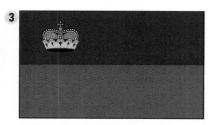

LIECHTENSTEIN LIECHTENSTEIN
EUROPE
Capital: **Vaduz**
Area: **160 km² (62 sq mi)** 191st
Population: **38,000** 190th
GDP: **$6.84B** 154th   Currency: **Franc (CHF)**
Highest Point: **Grauspitz (2620m)** 88th
Official Languages: **German**

LITHUANIA LIETUVA
EUROPE
Capital: **Vilnius**
Area: **65,300km² (25,200 sq mi)** 121st
Population: **2,722,000** 136th
GDP: **$62.2B** 78th   Currency: **Euro (EUR)**
Highest Point: **Aukstojas Hill (294m)** 177th
Official Languages: **Lithuanian**

1806 · 1815 · 1847 · 1951 · 1957/1960 · 1964 · 1965 · 1990

SOVEREIGNTY BY COUNTRY
●=Independence, ●=Formed

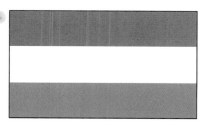

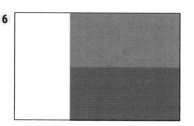

LUXEMBOURG LËTZEBUERG

Capital: **Luxembourg City**
Area: **2586km² (998 sq mi)** 169th
Population: **626,000** 164th
GDP: **$84.1B** 67th   Currency: **Euro (EUR)**
Highest Point: **Kneiff (560m)** 167th
Official Languages: **French/German/
Luxembourgish**

MADAGASCAR

AFRICA   MADAGASIKARA

Capital: **Antannarivo**
Area: **587,041km² (226,658 sq mi)** 45th
Population: **27,691,000** 52nd
GDP: **$14.8B** 124th   Currency: **Ariary (MGA)**
Highest Point: **Maromokotro (2876m)** 71st
Official Languages: **French/Malagasy**

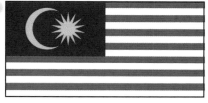

MALAWI MALAWI

AFRICA

Capital: **Lilongwe**
Area: **118,484 km² (45,747 sq mi)** 98th
Population: **19,130,000** 62nd
GDP: **$9.27B** 147th   Currency: **Kwacha (MWK)**
Highest Point: **Mt. Mulanje (3002m)** 62nd
Official Languages: **English/Chichewa**

MALAYSIA MALAYSIA

ASIA

Capital: **Kuala Lumpur**
Area: **330,803km² (127,754 sq mi)** 67th
Population: **32,365,000** 43rd
GDP: **$387B** 38th   Currency: **Ringgit (MYR)**
Highest Point: **Gunung Kinabalu (4095m)** 38th
Official Languages: **Malaysian**

MALDIVES

ASIA

Capital: **Male**
Area: **298 km² (115 sq mi)** 188th
Population: **541,000** 172nd
GDP: **$4.54B** 158th   Currency: **Rufiyaa (MVR)**
Highest Point: **Mt. Villingili (5m)** 191st
Official Languages: **Dhivehi/English**

MALI MALI

AFRICA

Capital: **Bamako**
Area: **1,240,192 km² (478,841 sq mi)** 23rd
Population: **20,251,000** 59th
GDP: **$19.9B** 118th   Currency: **Franc (XAF)**
Highest Point: **Hombori Tondo (1155m)** 142nd
Official Languages: **French**

MALTA MALTA

EUROPE

Capital: **Valetta**
Area: **316 km² (122 sq mi)** 187th
Population: **442,000** 168th
GDP: **$16.5B** 127th   Currency: **Euro (EUR)**
Highest Point: **Ta'Dmejrek (253m)** 178th
Official Languages: **English/Maltese**

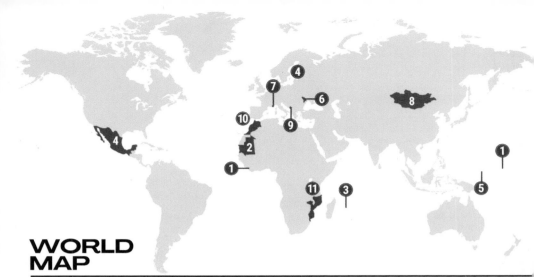

WORLD MAP

MARSHALL ISLANDS
AUS & OCEANIA   M̧AJEL̗
Capital: **Majuro**
Area: **181km² (70.1 sq mi)** 190th
Population: **59,000** 188th
GDP: **$234M** 191st   Currency: **Dollar (USD)**
Highest Point: **Unnamed (10m)** 190th
Official Languages: **English/Marshallese**

MAURITANIA موريتانيا
AFRICA
Capital: **Nouakchott**
Area: **1,030,000km² (400,000 sq mi)** 38th
Population: **4,660,000** 127th
GDP: **$9.24B** 148th   Currency: **Ouguiya (MRU**
Highest Point: **Keidet et Jill (915m)** 154th
Official Languages: **Arabic**

MAURITIUS MAURITIUS/MAURICE
AFRICA
Capital: **Port Louis**
Area: **2040km² (790 sq mi)** 170th
Population: **1,262,000** 155th
GDP: **$12.2B** 140th   Currency: **Rupee (MUR)**
Highest Point: **Piton de la Petite Riviere Noire (828m)** 160th
Official Languages: **(English/French)**

MEXICO MÉXICO
N. AMERICA
Capital: **Mexico City**
Area: **1,972,550km² (761,610 sq mi)** 13th
Population: **128,933,000** 10th
GDP: **$1.19T** 15th   Currency: **Peso (MXN)**
Highest Point: **Pico De Orizaba (5636m)** 20th
Official Languages: **(Spanish +68 others)**

1814 1821   1921   1956 1960 1968 1975 1986 1991   2006
7 **4**   **8**   **10** **2** **3** **11** **1** **6**   **9**

SOVEREIGNTY BY COUNTRY
●=Independence, ●=Forme

5

MICRONESIA MICRONESIA
AUS & OCEANIA
Capital: **Palikir**
Area: **702km² (271 sq mi)** 178th
Population: **115,000** 182nd
GDP: **$401M** 190th   Currency: **Dollar (USD)**
Highest Point: **Mt. Nanlaud (782m)** 161st
Official Languages: **English**

6

MOLDOVA MOLDOVA
EUROPE
Capital: **Chisinau**
Area: **33,846km² (13,068 sq mi)** 135th
Population: **4,034,000** 139th
GDP: **$12.0B** 142nd   Currency: **Leu (MDL)**
Highest Point: **Balanesti Hill (430m)** 169th
Official Languages: **Romanian**

7

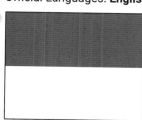

MONACO MONACO
EUROPE
Capital: **Monaco**
Area: **2.2km² (0.85 sq mi)** 195th
Population: **39,000** 191st
GDP: **$7.42B** 152nd   Currency: **Euro (EUR)**
Highest Point: **Unnamed (164m)** 182nd
Official Languages: **French**

8

MONGOLIA МОНГОЛ УЛС
ASIA
Capital: **Ulaanbaatar**
Area: **1,566,000 km² (605,000 sq mi)** 18th
Population: **3,278,000** 132nd
GDP: **$14.2B** 134th   Currency: **Tugrik (MNT)**
Highest Point: **Khuiten Peak (4374m)** 35th
Official Languages: **Mongolian**

9

MONTENEGRO CRNA GORA
EUROPE
Capital: **Podgorica**
Area: **13,812 km² (5333 sq mi)** 156th
Population: **628,000** 165th
GDP: **$5.65B** 154th   Currency: **Euro (EUR)**
Highest Point: **Zla Kolata (2534m)** 93rd
Official Languages: **Albanian/Bosnian/Croatian/ Montenegrin/Serbian**

10

MOROCCO المغرب/ⵍⵎⵖⵔⵉⴱ
AFRICA
Capital: **Al Rabat**
Area: **710,850km² (274,460 sq mi)** 57th
Population: **36,911,000** 39th
GDP: **$124B** 60th   Currency: **Dirham (MAD)**
Highest Point: **Jbel Toubkal (4165m)** 37th
Official Languages: **Arabic/Berber**

11

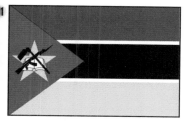

MOZAMBIQUE MOÇAMBIQUE
AFRICA
Capital: **Maputo**
Area: **801,590 km² (309,500 sq mi)** 35th
Population: **31,255,000** 47th
GDP: **$14.0B** 135th   Currency: **Metical (MZN)**
Highest Point: **Monte Binga (2436m)** 98th
Official Languages: **Portuguese**

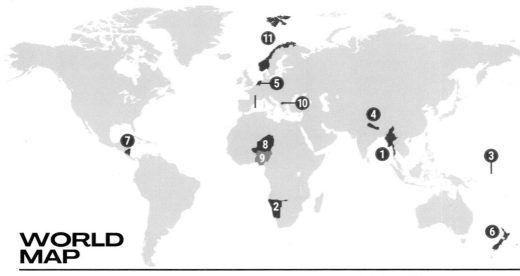

WORLD MAP

MYANMAR မြန်မာ

ASIA 🏵

Capital: **Naypyidaw**
Area: **676,578 km² (261,228 sq mi)** 39th
Population: **54,410,000** 26th
GDP: **$76.2B** 71st   Currency: **Kyat (MMK)**
Highest Point: **Hkakabo Razi (5881m)** 17th
Official Languages: **Burmese**

NAMIBIA NAMIBIA

AFRICA 🇳🇦

Capital: **Windhoek**
Area: **825,615km² (318,772 sq mi)** 34th
Population: **2,541,000** 140th
GDP: **$11.4B** 145th   Currency: **Dollar (NAD**
Highest Point: **Brandberg Mountain (2573m)** 90th
Official Languages: **English**

NAURU NAOERO

AUS & OCEANIA 🇳🇷

Capital: **Yaren**
Area: **21 km² (8.1 sq mi)** 194th
Population: **11,000** 194th
GDP: **$133M** 194th   Currency: **Dollar (AUD)**
Highest Point: **Command Ridge (71m)** 187th
Official Languages: **Nauruan**

NEPAL नेपाल

ASIA 🏵

Capital: **Kathmandu**
Area: **147,181 km² (56,827 sq mi)** 93rd
Population: **29,137,000** 48th
GDP: **$36.1B** 100th   Currency: **Rupee (NPR**
Highest Point: **Mt. Everest (8848m)** 1st ★
Official Languages: **Nepali**

MY
NO

NETHERLANDS, THE
EUROPE
NEDERLAND
Capital: **Amsterdam/The Hague**
Area: **41,543 km² (16,040 sq mi)** 131st
Population: **17,135,000** 66th
GDP: **$1.01T** 17th   Currency: **Euro (EUR)**
Highest Point: **Mt. Scenery (887m)** 156th
Official Languages: **Dutch**

NEW ZEALAND AOTEAROA
AUS & OCEANIA
Capital: **Wellington**
Area: **268,021km² (103,483 sq mi)** 75th
Population: **4,822,000** 120th
GDP: **$243B** 50th   Currency: **Dollar (NZD)**
Highest Point: **Mt. Cook (3724m)** 44th
Official Languages: **English/Maori**

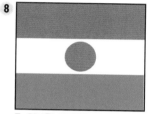

NICARAGUA NICARAGUA
N. AMERICA
Capital: **Managua**
Area: **130,375km² (50,338 sq mi)** 96th
Population: **6,625,000** 110th
GDP: **$12.3B** 138th   Currency: **Cordoba (NIO)**
Highest Point: **Mogoton (2107m)** 110th
Official Languages: **Spanish**

NIGER NIGER
AFRICA
Capital: **Niamey**
Area: **1,267,000km² (489,000 sq mi)** 21st
Population: **20,206,000** 56th
GDP: **$15.9B** 130th   Currency: **Franc (XOF)**
Highest Point: **Mont Idoukal-n-Taghes (2022m)** 115th
Official Languages: **French**

NIGERIA NIGERIA
AFRICA
Capital: **Abuja**
Area: **923,768 km² (356,669 sq mi)** 31st
Population: **206,140,000** 7th
GDP: **$514B** 27th   Currency: **Naira (NGN)**
Highest Point: **Chappal Waddi (2419m)** 99th
Official Languages: **English**

NORTH MACEDONIA
EUROPE   СЕВЕРНА МАКЕДОНИЈА
Capital: **Skopje**
Area: **25,713 km² (9928 sq mi)** 145th
Population: **2,083,000** 145th
GDP: **$13.8B** 136th   Currency: **Denar (MKD)**
Highest Point: **Golem Korab (2764m)** 79th
Official Languages: **Macedonian/Albanian**

NORWAY NORGE
EUROPE
Capital: **Oslo**
Area: **358,207 km² (148,729 sq mi)** 61st
Population: **5,421,000** 118th
GDP: **$445B** 31st   Currency: **Krone (NOK)**
Highest Point: **Galdhopiggen (2469m)** 96th
Official Languages: **Norweigan/Sami**

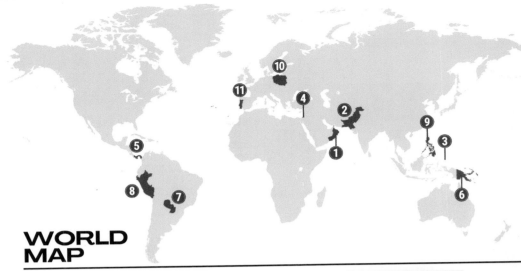

WORLD
MAP

OMAN عمان
ASIA ☪
Capital: **Muscat**
Area: **309,500 km² (119,500 sq mi)** 70th
Population: **5,107,000** 124th
GDP: **$74.1B** 73rd   Currency: **Rial (OMR)**
Highest Point: **Jabal Shams (3009m)** 59th
Official Languages: **Arabic**

PAKISTAN پاکستان
ASIA ☪
Capital: **Islamabad**
Area: **881,913 km² (340,509 sq mi)** 33rd
Population: **220,892,000** 5th
GDP: **$286B** 47th   Currency: **Rupee (PKI**
Highest Point: **K2 (8611m)** 2nd ★
Official Languages: **English/Urdu**

PALAU BELAU
AUS & OCEANIA ⌸
Capital: **Ngerulmud**
Area: **459 km² (177 sq mi)** 181st
Population: **18,000** 193rd
GDP: **$229M** 193rd   Currency: **Dollar (USD)**
Highest Point: **Mt. Ngelcherchuus (242m)** 179th
Official Languages: **English/Japanese/**
Palauan/Sonsorolese/Tobian

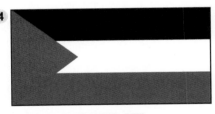

PALESTINE فلسطين
ASIA ☪
Capital: **Jerusalem**
Area: **6020km² (2320 sq mi)** 163rd
Population: **5,101,000** 122nd
GDP: **$16.8B** 126th   Currency: **Shekel (ILS**
Highest Point: **Mt. Nabi Yunis (1030m)** 148th
Official Languages: **Arabic**

SOVEREIGNT
BY COUNTR
● =Independence, ● =Form

PANAMA PANAMA
N. AMERICA
Capital: **Panama City**
Area: **75,417 km² (29,119 sq mi)** 40th
Population: **4,315,000** 126th
GDP: **$59.4B** 84th   Currency: **Dollar (USD)**
Highest Point: **Volcan Baru (3475m)** 49th
Official Languages: **Spanish**

PAPUA NEW GUINEA
AUS & OCEANIA   PAPUA NIUGINI
Capital: **Port Moresby**
Area: **462,840 km² (178,700 sq mi)** 54th
Population: **8,947,000** 97th
GDP: **$24.5B** 110th   Currency: **Kina (PGK)**
Highest Point: **Mt. Wilhelm (4509m)** 32nd
Official Languages: **English/Hiri Motu/
Tok Pisin**

PARAGUAY PARAGUAY
S. AMERICA
Capital: **Asuncion**
Area: **406,752km² (157,048 sq mi)** 59th
Population: **7,133,000** 102nd
GDP: **$37.8B** 97th   Currency: **Guarani (PYG)**
Highest Point: **Cerro Pero (3798m)** 158th
Official Languages: **Guarani/Spanish**

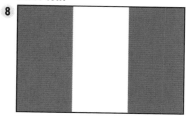

PERU PERU
S. AMERICA
Capital: **Lima**
Area: **1,285,216km² (496,225 sq mi)** 19th
Population: **32,972,000** 44th
GDP: **$226B** 51st   Currency: **Sol (PEN)**
Highest Point: **Huascaran (6768m)** 11th
Official Languages: **Spanish**

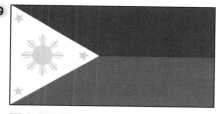

PHILIPPINES PILIPINAS
ASIA
Capital: **Manila**
Area: **300,000km² (115,000 sq mi)** 72nd
Population: **109,581,000** 12th
GDP: **$403B** 34th   Currency: **Peso (PHP)**
Highest Point: **Mt. Apo (2954m)** 67th
Official Languages: **English/Filipino**

POLAND POLSKA
EUROPE
Capital: **Warsaw**
Area: **312,696km² (120,733 sq mi)** 69th
Population: **37,847,000** 37th
GDP: **$642B** 22nd   Currency: **Zloty (PLN)**
Highest Point: **Ryzy (2499m)** 95th
Official Languages: **Polish**

PORTUGAL PORTUGAL
EUROPE
Capital: **Lisbon**
Area: **92,212km² (35,603 sq mi)** 109th
Population: **10,197,000** 89th
GDP: **$257B** 49th   Currency: **Euro (EUR)**
Highest Point: **Montanha Do Pico (2351m)** 102nd
Official Languages: **Portuguese**

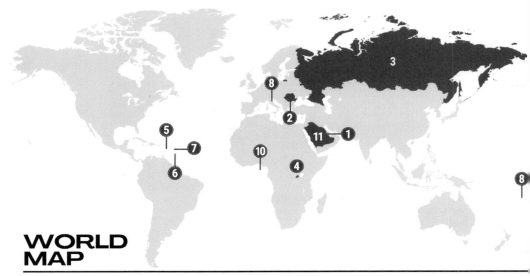

WORLD MAP

QATAR قطر
ASIA ⚫
Capital: **Doha**
Area: **11,581km² (4471 sq mi)** 158th
Population: **2,881,000** 137th
GDP: **$166B** 56th   Currency: **Riyal (QAR)**
Highest Point: **Qurayn Abu al Bawl (103m)** 184th
Official Languages: **Arabic**

ROMANIA ROMÂNIA
EUROPE ⚫
Capital: **Bucharest**
Area: **238,397km² (92,046 sq mi)** 81st
Population: **19,238,000** 61st
GDP: **$289B** 46th   Currency: **Leu (RON**
Highest Point: **Moldoveanu (2544m)** 92nd
Official Languages: **Romanian**

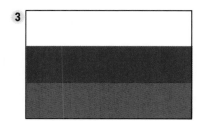

RUSSIA Россия
ASIA/EUROPE ⚫ (>20% landmass in both).
Capital: **Moscow**
Area: **17,098,246km² (6,601,670 sq mi)** 1st ★
Population: **145,934,000** 9th
GDP: **$1.71T** 11th   Currency: **Ruble (RUB)**
Highest Point: **Mt. Elbrus (5642m)** 19th
Official Languages: **Russian**

RWANDA U RWANDA
AFRICA ⚫
Capital: **Kigali**
Area: **26,338km² (10,169 sq mi)** 144th
Population: **12,952,000** 75th
GDP: **$10.6B** 146th   Currency: **Franc (RWF)**
Highest Point: **Mt. Karisimbi (4507m)** 33rd
Official Languages: **English/French/
Kinyarwanda/Swahili**

1243 ⑨ 1877 ② 1919 ⑪ **1962** ⑧ 1971 ① 1975 ⑩ **1979** ⑦ 1983 ⑤ 1991 ③

SOVEREIGNTY
BY COUNTRY
⚫ =Independence, ⚫ =Former

SAINT KITTS AND NEVIS
N. AMERICA ST. KITTS & NEVIS
Capital: **Basseterre**
Area: **261km² (101 sq mi)** 189th
Population: **53,000** 189th
GDP: **$831M** 184th   Currency: **Dollar (XCD)**
Highest Point: **Mt. Liamuiga (1156m)** 141st
Official Languages: **English**

SAINT LUCIA SAINT LUCIA
N. AMERICA
Capital: **Castries**
Area: **617km² (238 sq mi)** 179th
Population: **184,000** 178th
GDP: **$1.79B** 173rd   Currency: **Dollar (XCD)**
Highest Point: **Mt. Gimie (950m)** 152nd
Official Languages: **English**

SAINT VINCENT AND THE GRENADINES ST. VINCENT & THE GRENADINES
N. AMERICA
Capital: **Kingstown**
Area: **389 km² (150 sq mi)** 185th
Population: **111,000** 181st
GDP: **$798M** 185th   Currency: **Dollar (XCD)**
Highest Point: **La Soufriere (1234m)** 138th
Official Languages: **English**

SAMOA SĀMOA
AUS & OCEANIA
Capital: **Apia**
Area: **2842km² (1097 sq mi)** 168th
Population: **198,000** 177th
GDP: **$752M** 186th   Currency: **Tala (WST)**
Highest Point: **Mauga Silisili (1857m)** 123rd
Official Languages: **English/Samoan**

SAN MARINO SAN MARINO
EUROPE
Capital: **San Marino**
Area: **61km² (24 sq mi)** 192nd
Population: **34,000** 192nd
GDP: **$1.69B** 176th   Currency: **Euro (EUR)**
Highest Point: **Monte Titano (755m)** 162nd
Official Languages: **Italian**

SÃO TOMÉ AND PRÍNCIPE
AFRICA SÃO TOMÉ AND PRÍNCIPE
Capital: **Sao Tome**
Area: **1001km² (386 sq mi)** 172nd
Population: **219,000** 176th
GDP: **$485M** 189th   Currency: **Dobra (STN)**
Highest Point: **Pico de Sao Tome (2024m)** 114th
Official Languages: **Portuguese**

SAUDI ARABIA العربية السعودية
ASIA
Capital: **Riyadh**
Area: **2,149,690km² (830,000 sq mi)** 12th
Population: **33,000,000** 41st
GDP: **$805B** 19th   Currency: **Riyal (SAR)**
Highest Point: **Jabal Sawda (3000m)** 63rd
Official Languages: **Arabic**

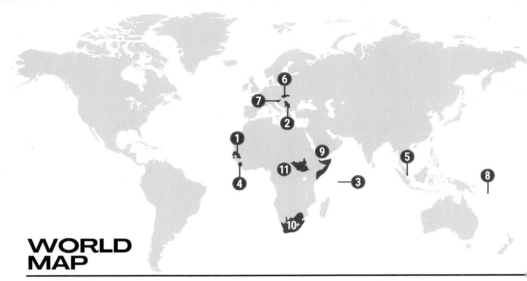

WORLD MAP

SENEGAL SÉNÉGAL
AFRICA 🌍
Capital: **Dakar**
Area: **196,712km² (75,951 sq mi)** 86th
Population: **16,744,000** 69th
GDP: **$27.9B** 103rd   Currency: **Franc (XOF)**
Highest Point: **Unnamed (648m)** 166th
Official Languages: **French**

SERBIA SRBIJA
EUROPE 🏴
Capital: **Belgrade**
Area: **88,361km² (34,116 sq mi)** 111th
Population: **8,737,000** 105th
GDP: **$60.4B** 82nd   Currency: **Dinar (RSI**
Highest Point: **Midzor (2169m)** 108th
Official Languages: **Serbian**

SEYCHELLES SEYCHELLES
AFRICA 🏴
Capital: **Victoria**
Area: **459km² (177 sq mi)** 182nd
Population: **98,000** 184th
GDP: **$948M** 182nd   Currency: **Rupee (SCR)**
Highest Point: **Morne Seychellois (905m)** 155th
Official Languages: **English/French/
Seychellois Creole**

SIERRA LEONE
AFRICA 🌍   SIERRA LEONE
Capital: **Freetown**
Area: **71,740km² (27,700 sq mi)** 117th
Population: **7,977,000** 100th
GDP: **$4.22B** 160th   Currency: **Leone (SLL)**
Highest Point: **Mt. Bintumani (1948m)** 119th
Official Languages: **English**

SOVEREIGNT
BY COUNTR
● =Independence, ● =Forme

SINGAPORE SINGAPORE
ASIA
Capital: **Singapore**
Area: **723km² (279 sq mi)** 177th
Population: **5,850,000** 113th
GDP: **$374B** 39th Currency: **Dollar (SGD)**
Highest Point: **Bukit Timah Hill (164m)** 181st
Official Languages: **Chinese/English/Malay /Tamil**

SLOVAKIA SLOVENSKO
EUROPE
Capital: **Bratislava**
Area: **49,035km² (18,933 sq mi)** 127th
Population: **5,460,000** 117th
GDP: **$117B** 61st Currency: **Euro (EUR)**
Highest Point: **Gerlachovsky Stit (2655m)** 85th
Official Languages: **Slovak**

SLOVENIA SLOVENIJA
EUROPE
Capital: **Ljubljana**
Area: **20,273km² (7827 sq mi)** 150th
Population: **2,079,000** 144th
GDP: **$59.1B** 85th Currency: **Euro (EUR)**
Highest Point: **Triglav (2864m)** 73rd
Official Languages: **Slovene**

SOLOMON ISLANDS
AUS & OCEANIA SOLOMON ISLANDS
Capital: **Honiara**
Area: **28,400km² (11,000 sq mi)** 139th
Population: **687,000** 163rd
GDP: **$1.64B** 178th Currency: **Dollar (SBD)**
Highest Point: **Mt. Popomanaseu (2335m)** 103rd
Official Languages: **English**

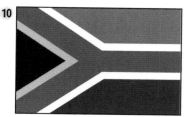

SOMALIA SOOMAALIYA/الصومال
AFRICA
Capital: **Mogadishu**
Area: **637,657km² (246,201 sq mi)** 43rd
Population: **15,893,000** 71st
GDP: **$5.37B** 155th Currency: **Shilling (SOS)**
Highest Point: **Shimbiris (2450m)** 97th
Official Languages: **Arabic/Somali**

SOUTH AFRICA
AFRICA SOUTH AFRICA
Capital: **Bloemfontein/Cape Town/Pretoria**
Area: **1,221,037km² (471,445 sq mi)** 24th
Population: **59,309,000** 24th
GDP: **$330B** 42nd Currency: **Rand (ZAR)**
Highest Point: **Mafadi (3450m)** 50th
Official Languages: **English +11 others**

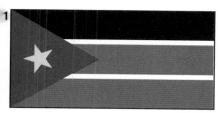

SOUTH SUDAN
AFRICA SUDAN KUSINI
Capital: **Juba**
Area: **619,745km² (239,285 sq mi)** 41st
Population: **11,194,000** 74th
GDP: **$4.46B** 159th Currency: **Pound (SSP)**
Highest Point: **Kinyeti (3187m)** 52nd
Official Languages: **English/Swahili**

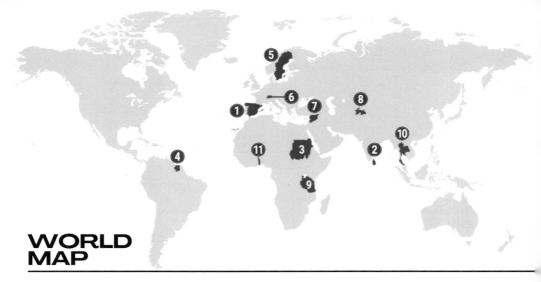

WORLD MAP

SPAIN ESPAÑA
EUROPE 🇪🇸
Capital: **Madrid**
Area: **505,990km² (195,360 sq mi)** 51st
Population: **46,755,000** 30th
GDP: **$1.46T** 14th   Currency: **Euro (EUR)**
Highest Point: **Teide (3718m)** 45th
Official Languages: **Spanish**

SRI LANKA
ASIA 🇱🇰 ශ්‍රී ලංකා/இலங்கை
Capital: **Colombo/Sri Jayawardenepura Kotte**
Area: **65,610km² (25,330 sq mi)** 120th
Population: **21,413,000** 57th
GDP: **$84.5B** 66th   Currency: **Rupee (LKR)**
Highest Point: **Pidurutalagala (2524m)** 94th
Official Languages: **Sinhala/Tamil**

SUDAN SUDAN/السودان
AFRICA 🇸🇩
Capital: **Khartoum**
Area: **1,886,068km² (728,215 sq mi)** 15th
Population: **43,849,000** 33rd
GDP: **$35.8B** 101st   Currency: **Pound (SDG)**
Highest Point: **Deriba Caldera (3042m)** 57th
Official Languages: **Arabic/English**

SURINAME SURINAME
S. AMERICA 🇸🇷
Capital: **Paramaribo**
Area: **163,821km² (63,252 sq mi)** 90th
Population: **587,000** 166th
GDP: **$2.47B** 168th   Currency: **Dollar (SRD)**
Highest Point: **Juliana Top (1230m)** 139th
Official Languages: **Dutch**

1238 1516 1523 1648   1946 1948   1956 1960 1961   1975   1991

 10 1 5 6    7 2   3 11 9   4   8

SOVEREIGNTY BY COUNTRY
⬤ =Independence, ⬤ =Forme

SWEDEN SVERIGE
EUROPE
Capital: **Stockholm**
Area: **450,295km² (173,860 sq mi)** 55th
Population: **10,099,000** 88th
GDP: **$626B** 23rd Currency: **Krona (SEK)**
Highest Point: **Kebnekaise (2097m)** 111th
Official Languages: **Swedish**

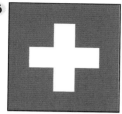

SWITZERLAND
EUROPE   SUISSE/DER SCHWEIZ/
SVIZZERA/SVIZRA
Capital: **Bern**
Area: **41,285km² (15,940 sq mi)** 132nd
Population: **8,655,000** 99th
GDP: **$825B** 18th Currency: **Franc (CHF)**
Highest Point: **Dufourspitze (4634m)** 30th
Official Languages: **French/German/Italian/
Romansh**

SYRIA سوريا
ASIA
Capital: **Damascus**
Area: **185,180km² (71,500 sq mi)** 87th
Population: **17,501,000** 67th
GDP: **$20.0B** 117th Currency: **Pound (SYP)**
Highest Point: **Jabal El-Sheikh (2814m)** 76th
Official Languages: **Arabic**

TAJIKISTAN ТОҶИКИСТОН
ASIA
Capital: **Dushanbe**
Area: **143,100km² (55,300 sq mi)** 94th
Population: **9,538,000** 94th
GDP: **$7.83B** 151st Currency: **Somoni (TJS)**
Highest Point: **Ismoil Somoni Peak (7495m)** 5th
Official Languages: **Tajik**

TANZANIA TANZANIA
AFRICA
Capital: **Dar Es Saleem**
Area: **947,303km² (365,756 sq mi)** 30th
Population: **59,734,000** 25th
GDP: **$65.9B** 76th Currency: **Shilling (TZS)**
Highest Point: **Kilimanjaro (5892m)** 16th
Official Languages: **Arabic/English/Swahili**

THAILAND ประเทศไทย
ASIA
Capital: **Bangkok**
Area: **513,120km² (198,120 sq mi)** 50th
Population: **69,800,000** 22nd
GDP: **$539B** 25th Currency: **Baht (THB)**
Highest Point: **Doi Inthanon (2565m)** 91st
Official Languages: **Thai**

TOGO TOGO
AFRICA FOLK
Capital: **Lome**
Area: **56,785km² (21,925 sq mi)** 123rd
Population: **8,278,000** 101st
GDP: **$8.63B** 150th Currency: **Franc (XOF)**
Highest Point: **Mont Agou (986m)** 151st
Official Languages: **French**

35

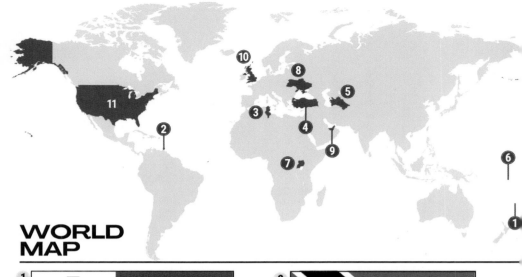

WORLD MAP

TONGA TONGA
AUS & OCEANIA 🏳

Capital: **Nuku'alofa**
Area: **748km² (289 sq mi)** 176th
Population: **106,000** 183rd
GDP: **$508M** 188th   Currency: **Pa'anga (TOP)**
Highest Point: **Unnamed (1033m)** 147th
Official Languages: **English/Tongan**

TRINIDAD AND TOBAGO
N. AMERICA 🏳   TRINIDAD & TOBAGO

Capital: **Port Of Spain**
Area: **5131 km² (1981 sq mi)** 166th
Population: **1,399,000** 152nd
GDP: **$22.2B** 114th   Currency: **Dollar (TTD)**
Highest Point: **El Cerro del Aripo (940m)** 153rd
Official Languages: **English**

TUNISIA تونس
AFRICA 🔄

Capital: **Tunis**
Area: **163,610km² (63,170 sq mi)** 91st
Population: **11,819,000** 79th
GDP: **$44.3B** 92nd   Currency: **Dinar (TND)**
Highest Point: **Jebel ech Chambi (1544m)** 130th
Official Languages: **Arabic**

TURKEY TÜRKIYE
ASIA 🔄

Capital: **Ankara**
Area: **783,356km² (302,455 sq mi)** 36th
Population: **84,339,000** 19th
GDP: **$795B** 20th   Currency: **Lira (TRY)**
Highest Point: **Mt. Ararat (5137m)** 24th
Official Languages: **Turkish**

1707 1776   1923   1956 1962   1970 1971   1978   1991
10 11   4   3 2   1 9   6   8 5

SOVEREIGNTY BY COUNTRY
●=Independence, ●=Former

TURKMENISTAN
ASIA TÜRKMENISTAN
Capital: **Ashgabat**
Area: **491,210km² (189,660 sq mi)** 52nd
Population: **6,031,000** 111th
GDP: **$54.2B** 88th   Currency: **Manat (TMT)**
Highest Point: **Ayrybaba (3139m)** 54th
Official Languages: **Turkmen**

TO UN

TUVALU TUVALU
AUS & OCEANIA
Capital: **Funafuti**
Area: **26km² (10 sq mi)** 193rd
Population: **12,000** 195th
GDP: **$57.0M** 195th   Currency: **Dollar (AUD)**
Highest Point: **Unnamed (5m)** 192nd
Official Languages: **English/Tuvaluan**

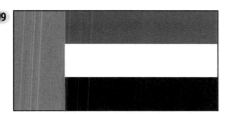

UGANDA UGANDA
AFRICA
Capital: **Kampala**
Area: **241,038km² (93,065 sq mi)** 79th
Population: **45,741,000** 35th
GDP: **$41.3B** 95th   Currency: **Shilling (UGX)**
Highest Point: **Mt. Stanley (5109m)** 25th
Official Languages: **English/Swahili**

UKRAINE УКРАЇНА
EUROPE
Capital: **Kiev**
Area: **576,500km² (222,600 sq mi)** 48th
Population: **43,733,000** 34th
GDP: **$165B** 57th   Currency: **Hryvnia (UAH)**
Highest Point: **Hoverla (2061m)** 112th
Official Languages: **Ukrainian**

UNITED ARAB EMIRATES
ASIA الإمارات العربية المتحدة
Capital: **Abu Dhabi**
Area: **83,600km² (32,300 sq mi)** 114th
Population: **9,890,000** 91st
GDP: **$402B** 35th   Currency: **Dirham (AED)**
Highest Point: **Jabal Al Jais (1910m)** 120th
Official Languages: **Arabic**

UNITED KINGDOM
EUROPE UNITED KINGDOM
Capital: **London**
Area: **242,495 km² (93,628 sq mi)** 78th
Population: **67,886,000** 21st
GDP: **$3.12T** 5th   Currency: **Pound (GBP)**
Highest Point: **Ben Nevis (1345m)** 135th
Official Languages: **English**

UNITED STATES UNITED STATES
N. AMERICA
Capital: **Washington D.C.**
Area: **9,833,520km² (3,796,742 sq mi)** 3rd ★
Population: **331,003,000** 3rd ★
GDP: **$22.7T** 1st ★   Currency: **Dollar (USD)**
Highest Point: **Denali (6191m)** 14th
Official Languages: **(English)**

WORLD MAP

URUGUAY URUGUAY
S. AMERICA 🏳
Capital: **Montevideo**
Area: **176,215km² (68,037 sq mi)** 89th
Population: **3,474,000** 131st
GDP: **$55.5B** 86th   Currency: **Peso (UYU)**
Highest Point: **Cerro Catedral (514m)** 168th
Official Languages: **Spanish**

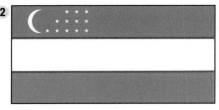

UZBEKISTAN O'ZBEKISTON
ASIA ☪
Capital: **Tashkent**
Area: **448,798 km² (173,351 sq mi)** 56th
Population: **33,469,000** 40th
GDP: **$61.2B** 79th   Currency: **Som (UZS)**
Highest Point: **Khazret Sultan (4643m)** 29th
Official Languages: **Uzbek**

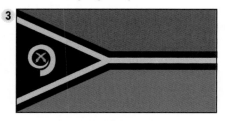

VANUATU VANUATU
AUS & OCEANIA 🏳
Capital: **Port Vila**
Area: **12,189 km² (4,706 sq mi)** 157th
Population: **307,000** 174th
GDP: **$912M** 183rd   Currency: **Vatu (VUV)**
Highest Point: **Mt. Tabwemasana (1877m)** 121st
Official Languages: **Bislama/English/French**

VATICAN CITY
EUROPE 🏳   CITTÀ DEL VATICANO
Capital: **Vatican City**
Area: **0.4km² (0.2 sq mi)** 196th
Population: **830** 196th
GDP: -   Currency: **Euro (EUR)**
Highest Point: **Vatican Hill (75m)** 186th
Official Languages: **Italian/Latin**

1811	1828	1918	1929	1945	1964	1980	1991
5	1	7	4	6	8	3	2

SOVEREIGNTY BY COUNTRY
● =Independence, ● =Former

5

VENEZUELA VENEZUELA
S. AMERICA
Capital: **Caracas**
Area: **916,445km²(353,841 sq mi)** 32nd
Population: **28,436,000** 50th
GDP: **$42.5B** 94th   Currency: **Bolivar (VES)**
Highest Point: **Pico Bolivar (4978m)** 26th
Official Languages: **Spanish**

6

VIETNAM VIỆT NAM
ASIA
Capital: **Hanoi**
Area: **331,212 km²(127,882 sq mi)** 66th
Population: **97,339,000** 15th
GDP: **$355B** 41st   Currency: **Dong (VND)**
Highest Point: **Fan Si Pan (3143m)** 53rd
Official Languages: **(Vietnamese)**

7

YEMEN اَلْيَمَن
ASIA
Capital: **Sana'a**
Area: **527,968 km² (203,850 sq mi)** 49th
Population: **29,825,000** 49th
GDP: **$25.1B** 109th   Currency: **Rial (YER)**
Highest Point: **Jabal An-Nabi Shu'ayb (3666m)** 46th
Official Languages: **Arabic**

8

ZAMBIA ZAMBIA
AFRICA
Capital: **Lusaka**
Area: **752,618 km²(290,587 sq mi)** 38th
Population: **18,384,000** 64th
GDP: **$19.0B** 120th Currency: **Kwacha (ZMW)**
Highest Point: **Magfina Central (2329m)** 104th
Official Languages: **English**

9

ZIMBABWE ZIMBABWE
AFRICA
Capital: **Harare**
Area: **390,757km²(150,872 sq mi)** 60th
Population: **14,863,000** 72nd
GDP: **$26.1B** 108th   Currency: **Dollar (USD)**
Highest Point: **Mt. Nyangani (2592m)** 89th
Official Languages: **English (+16 others)**

MISCELLANEOUS FLAGS
TERRITORIES NOT REPRESENTED BY A COUNTRY ABOVE

GREENLAND KALAALLIT NUNAAT
Capital: **Nuuk**
Area: **2,166,086km² (836,330 sq mi)**
Population: **56,000**
GDP: - Currency: **Krone (DKK)**
Highest Point: **Gunnbjørn Fjeld (3694m)**
Official Languages: **Greenlandic**

REP. OF CHINA (TAIWAN)
台灣
Capital: **Taipei**
Area: **36,197km² (13,976 sq mi)**
Population: **23,781,000**
GDP: **$689B** Currency: **Dollar (TWD)**
Highest Point: **Yu Shan (3952m)**
Official Languages: **(Mandarin/Hakka)**

COUNTRIES WITHIN THE UNITED KINGDOM

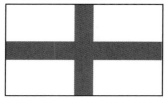

ENGLAND ENGLAND
Capital: **London**
Area: **130,279km² (50,301 sq mi)**
Population: **56,287,000**
Highest Point: **Scafell Pike (978m)**
Official Languages: **English**

WALES CYMRU
Capital: **Cardiff**
Area: **20,779km² (8,023 sq mi)**
Population: **3,153,000**
Highest Point: **Snowdon (1085m)**
Official Languages: **English/Welsh**

SCOTLAND ALBA
Capital: **Edinburgh**
Area: **77,933km² (30,090 sq mi)**
Population: **5,463,000**
Highest Point: **Ben Nevis (1345m**
Official Languages: **(English/
Scots/Scottish Gaelic)**

*

NORTHERN IRELAND
TUAISCEART ÉIREANN/NORLIN AIRLANN
Capital: **Belfast**
Area: **14,130km² (5,460 sq mi)**
Population: **1,894,000**
Highest Point: **Slieve Donard (850m)**
Official Languages: **(English/Irish/Ulster Scots)**
*The Ulster Banner and Union Jack are also flags
used to represent Northern Ireland

ORGANISATIONAL FLAGS

NATO

COMMONWEA-
LTH OF NATIONS

UNITED
NATIONS

EUROPEAN
UNION

AFRICAN
UNION

ARAB
LEAGUE

Printed in Great Britain
by Amazon

83442016R00025